THE SUPERHEROES EMPLOYMENT AGENCY

by MARILYN SINGER

Illustrated by

NOAH Z. JONES

CLARION BOOKS
Houghton Mifflin Harcourt
Boston   New York   2012

OPEN

SUPERHEROES EMPLOYMENT AGENCY

You folks all root for Superman,
his each and every quest.
Wonder Woman, Spidey, Hulk,
they're cheered from east to west.
Well, here at S.E.A., my friend,
though right now you can't name us,
we're really proud of our own crowd—
and someday we'll be famous.

We're B-list superheroes.

You've never heard of us.

We're B-list superheroes,

but our talents are A-plus!

Foil a foul villain?

Control a hostile mob?

We'll send a superhero

who's perfect for the job.

No task's too small or hard.

We're always on alert.

(Pay now by credit card—

you'll get a free T-shirt!)

We bring stinkers to their knees.

(Check our contract and our fees.)

You need help without delay?

We're here for you. We're S.E.A.!

BLUNDER WOMAN

C.E.O. of the Superheroes Employment Agency

Wherever I worked,

assisted, or clerked,

without lifting a hand,

by a mental command,

I'd make hard drives expire

and phones go haywire.

I might flatten a tire

or ignite a small fire

to watch villains perspire

as I wrecked their empire

through each deliberate error

(my sly reign of terror).

I was never detected.

I was never respected.

I protected good folk—

but I nearly went broke . . .

So I began this agency

for superheroes just like me:

outclassed, outranked, unsung,

standing on the second rung.

Now we're proud and confident

(and I can pay my monthly rent).

THE VERMINATOR

A wall? Nothing to it.

I walk straight on through it,

interfering with its matter,

causing molecules to scatter,

be it wood or brick or plaster,

concrete, steel, or alabaster,

granite, fiberglass, or bronze.

Into bank vaults and salons,

into offices and labs,

armored trucks and cruising cabs,

I will enter for a price

to do a job on rats and mice,

make their neurons go awry.

They're *auf Wiedersehen*, goodbye!

For thugs, you've got the Terminator.

For rodents, me, the Verminator.

Fleas and roaches (American or German)

fall to the Verminator (real name: Herman).

So what if I am just an inch?

I don't falter. I don't flinch.

Remember, when the need arises:

Superheroes come in many sizes.

CALL ON MUFFY THE VAMPIRE SPRAYER
FOR THE BEST PEST CONTROL IN TOWN.
CALL ON MUFFY THE VAMPIRE SPRAYER,
'CAUSE MUFFY BRINGS 'EM DOWN.

SHE CAN WALK THE WALK.
SHE CAN TALK THE TALK.
AND BELIEVE US, BROTHER,
SHE CAN CAULK THE CAULK.

VAMPIRES INSIDE? *PFFT,* SHE'LL ROUT 'EM!
VAMPIRES OUTSIDE? *PFFT,* SHE'LL GROUT 'EM.

Wake me up when she's gone!

24-HOUR SERVICE.

TRUST OUR SLOGAN:
YOU DESERVE US.

BOO!

(AND REMEMBER, FOR SMALLER VERMIN,
GET THE VERMINATOR, HERMAN.)

CLAIRVOYANT'S LAMENT

It's true that I've made lots of money.
It's true that I've been a success.
It's true that I know how to read minds—
It's true that I don't need to guess.

But I'd give up my entire fortune,
right down to my very last cent,
if I could do something quite different.
Dear clients, please hear my lament:

I know what you want before you want it.
I know what you'll get before you do.
I know when you'll find something boring.
I know when you'll want something new.

I know where to send you to find it,
to places where no one yet goes.
I know what you think makes you happy,
be it comic books, model cars, clothes.

I know how you could be a hero
and how you could learn to be kind.
I know how to make the world better . . .
but I can't get that into your mind!

CAJOLER

I can convince them. I can persuade
a dog to give up his bone,
a king to give up his throne.

I can be charming and I can enchant
a kid to like mushy peas,
a guard to give me his keys.

But what is the outcome?
I never can tell.
I know that they're buying,
but what did I sell?
Will coaxing make everything fine?
Will someone improve or decline?
Telepathy isn't my line.
I wish I were psychic.

Now, that
would be swell!

REPORT:
THE PRETZEL

The prizewinning scientist
  Kelvin O. Rem
discovered the secret
  of Element M—

when a tiny amount is combined
  with a laser
in a handy device that resembles
  a razor

that you click with a flick
  to set it on stun,
it will instantly make
  anyone weigh a ton,

unable to amble,
  unable to trudge,
unable, in fact,
  to stand up or budge.

Imagine the power
  this weapon would bring!
Imagine the villains
  who longed for that thing!

The Gamma Ray Gang,
  the worst of the worst,
came up with a scheme
  to get to Rem first.

While he was at work,
    they broke into his house,
took hostage his beagle,
    two kids, and his spouse,

and threatened to dish out
    a fate oh so cruel
if Rem didn't give them
    that dangerous tool.

But the man's good assistant
    was able to phone us.
(I hope Dr. Rem gives that woman
    a bonus.)

What hero could give those bad Gammas
    a flattening?
What hero would fight with his might
    against fattening?

13

We summoned the Pretzel,
   who squeezed through the transom
and freed those poor Rems
   being held there for ransom.

The Gamma Ray gangsters
   could fire no shots—
our hero had tied them
   in multiple knots.

The safe and sound Rems
    were grateful until
the day they received
    an extreme cleaning bill.

The truth must be told:
    it's the Pretzel's own fault
that our clients' neat home
    got so sprinkled with salt.

On sofas and rugs,
    on curtains and bedding,
our flexible hero
    was constantly shedding.

He's fearless and brilliant
    with menacing mobs.
But from now on let's send him
    on just *outdoor* jobs.

WEATHERGIRL (A.K.A. Cyclone)

From up in space to down in Hades,
there are villains who are ladies.
They wear white gloves and fancy hats.
They like to knit. They're fond of cats.
They're always planning something sinister
against a monarch or prime minister
over cake and cups of tea.
But then they have to deal with me,
a welcome guest, one of their ilk,
spooning sugar, pouring milk,
until my powers spoil their plot.
I raise a storm in their teapot.
Before they even utter, "Darn,"
I wrap them tightly in their yarn.
Then—*whoosh!*—I blow each one away,
still sopping wet from their Earl Grey.

SEND THE BABY!

When thieves are plotting and need silence
and you'd prefer to not use violence,
send the Baby, send the Baby.

When racketeers insist on quiet
and it's not wise to start a riot,
send the Baby, send the Baby.

The toughest gangsters always quail
when our tot begins to wail.
They roll their eyes, they tear their hair.
They soon run screaming from their lair.

And if those cries don't make them hyper,
Weapon Two is in the diaper.
Send the Baby, send the Baby.

Send the Baby . . . now!

HERK/ULEEZ

They're champions who specialize.

Herk and Uleez are your guys.

One lifts up cars (and also washes 'em).

One lets 'em drop (and also squashes 'em).

One saves victims who are trapped.

One trashes cars until they're scrapped.

Both can cause a mean gridlock

when you need chaos on your block.

They'll battle for the common good—

but also conquer Hollywood.

No need to waste dough on special effects

in films that feature colossal car wrecks—

these muscular twins will make it look real.

And two for one price—now, you know that's a steal!

Yes, Herk and Uleez are your guys.

They're champions who specialize.

STUPORMAN

You know that dude built like an ape?
Can leap and fly in tights and cape?
Nickname is the Man of Steel?
Trust me, kid, he's no big deal.
Bad guys? I don't need a punch
to incapacitate the bunch.
I just recite my epic poem
or chapters from my latest tome
or several acts from my new plays,
and—presto!—their eyes start to glaze.
I've essays and reports galore
I guarantee will make them snore.
Yes, indeed, my power's super:
I put villains in a stupor.
You don't believe me? Then listen, please:
"Chapter Ninety-One: How to Eat
        Cottage Cheese."

THE BULK

My notorious cousin, the Hulk,

so very green and large,

is inclined to bust things up when he gets mad.

I'm rarely angry. I seldom fume.

I never, ever charge.

Rather, I get happy-sappy-sad.

I think of babies, kitties, pups,

and I begin to sigh.

I swell up like a sponge filled with emotion.

I give myself a little squeeze,

and then I start to cry,

and pretty soon those drops become an ocean.

But, brother, I am more

than just a sentimental dude.

I'm the stuff of all you tyrants'

biggest fears.

So, you creeps who call me sissy

better fix your attitude

or I'll *dissolve* you lot

in endless floods of tears.

I'm the Bulk. Oh, yes, indeed.

I'm so fond of darling creatures I can cuddle.

I'm the Bulk. Foul fiends, take heed

or you'll wind up floating in a giant puddle.

A Former Member of the Justice League
(KELLY)

I was in Green Lantern's corps.

On evildoers we waged war.

Together we would travel time.

We'd fly, read minds, and battle crime.

Our famous rings produced a ray

that let us go and save the day.

A light against darkness—that was our creed.

Regrettably, I disagreed

with several members concerning its tint.

They claimed it was lime. I swore it was mint.

We argued so about the beam,

I had to quit Green Lantern's team.

I'm here because I need to find

a boss who isn't colorblind.

What's that you say? You're not for real!

There's *no* way that this shade is **TEAL!**

THE CATERPILLAR

Clinging, crawling, spinning silk.
There is no one of my ilk.
I can wrap a thug or goon
in a rather snug cocoon.
But it's gotten a bit dreary.
I would like a job more cheery.
What I want is to design,
to create a special line
for your employees to wear,
things that will not shred or tear;
costumes for each gal and guy,
to make each a butterfly.
We could open a boutique.
Superheroes should look chic!

REPORT:
METAMORPH

At Clooney School, young Wilfrid Wilde
was clearly quite a problem child.

He threw a ball at Matthew's head
and took Elena's cookie money.
He ate Tim's sandwich (left the bread)
and smeared Ms. Dexter's desk with honey.

Ms. D., the teacher, was disgusted.
Could we get him bully-busted?

When predicaments are pressing,
there's no agency that's swifter.
With Will's parents' timely blessing,
we directed our shape-shifter,

Metamorph, to pay a visit
and put that Wilde child in a trance.
Then, using talent so exquisite,
(plus his shirt and shoes and pants),

she became his perfect double
and went to school to fix the trouble.

That day, Wilfrid Wilde seemed strange.
He cheered when Matthew scored in gym.
He offered Mary Beth his change
and shared his mac and cheese with Tim.

For one whole month he stayed a darling.
Didn't trip kids in the aisle.
No more shoving, no more snarling.
Came in humming, with a smile.

To:the
kid I used
to beat
up

Yesterday at nine o'clock,
the real young Will got quite a shock

when he returned to Clooney School
and kids and teachers all said, "Hi!"
They seemed to think that he was cool.
It looked as if they liked the guy.

we love
Wilfrid

Though Wilfrid doesn't get it, fully,
we report a happy end.
It's way too hard to stay a bully
when everybody is your friend.

Reformed Bully

Problem people got you down?
Don't mope on the nearest wharf.
This genius will erase your frown—
our one and only

KELLY and THE CATERPILLAR

KELLY and THE CATERPILLAR

For Trendy Defenders

Want to look better?
Be a trendsetter?

Whether it's

whiz, whoosh, boom, or **pow,**

we make sure your style is

NOW.

NOT REALLY BATMAN

Gimme money, money, money,

and a really fancy car,

a manor and a butler,

and I too would be a star.

Gimme every kind of gadget

to fight crime and then escape

(I've already got the mask;

I already own the cape),

and I'd be Batman,

standing brave and tall.

Batman,

beloved by (nearly) all.

Batman!

Always there on call.

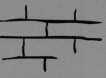

Not just an actor

who plays him at the mall.

With some training and big dough,

I'd be a superhero, bro.

My foes would all be sobbin'

if you also toss in Robin.

I would be Batman . . .

What do you mean, "leave"?

Come on, you can't throw me out . . .

Don't you know who I . . . could be . . . ?

Batman!

That could be me!

All right, all right, I'm going . . .

GOODBYE FROM OUR C.E.O.

Now that you have met our crew,
it's clear that we're incredible.
You didn't know us yesterday—
today, we're unforgettable!

We're not in graphic novels.
We're not in comic books.
But we stop villains in their tracks.
We catch thugs and crooks.

We help good folks everywhere,
on land, in air, at sea.
(Hire us eleven times—
the twelfth job's always free!)

For endurance, smarts, and speed
(and a sense of fashion, too),
S.E.A.'s got what you need—
we're always here for you!

BLUNDER
WOMAN
C.E.UH-OH.

To my super
nephew, Asher
—M.S.

For my dad,
who has always
been a super guy,
even if he does
look silly in a
cape and tights
—N.Z.J.

Clarion Books
215 Park Avenue South, New York, New York 10003

Text copyright © 2012 by Marilyn Singer
Illustrations copyright © 2012 by Noah Z. Jones

Clarion Books is an imprint of Houghton Mifflin Harcourt Publishing Company.

www.hmhbooks.com

The text of this book was set in Bryant, Sweater School, and Humper.
The illustrations were executed digitally.
Book design by Sharismar Rodriguez

Library of Congress Cataloging-in-Publication Data
Singer, Marilyn.
The superheroes employment agency / by Marilyn Singer ; illustrated by Noah Z. Jones.
p. cm.
ISBN 978-0-547-43559-6
1. Superheroes—Juvenile poetry. I. Jones, Noah (Noah Z.) ill. II. Title.
PS3569.I546S87 2011
811'.54—dc23   2011025722

Manufactured in Singapore
TWP 10 9 8 7 6 5 4 3 2 1
4500353926